The Muscular System

by Helen Frost

Consulting Editor: Gail Saunders-Smith, Ph.D.

Consultant: Lawrence M. Ross, M.D., Ph.D.
Member, American Association of Clinical Anatomists

Pebble Books

an imprint of Capstone Press
Mankato, Minnesota

Pebble Books are published by Capstone Press
151 Good Counsel Drive, P.O. Box 669, Mankato, Minnesota 56002
http://www.capstone-press.com

2 3 4 5 6 06 05 04 03 02

Library of Congress Cataloging-in-Publication Data
Frost, Helen, 1949–
    The muscular system / by Helen Frost.
    p. cm.—(Human body systems)
    Summary: Simple text, photographs, and diagrams introduce the muscular system and its purpose, parts, and functions.
    ISBN 0-7368-0650-4 (hardcover)
    ISBN 0-7368-8778-4 (paperback)
    1. Muscles—Juvenile literature. [1. Muscular system. 2. Muscles.] I. Title. II. Human body systems (Mankato, Minn.)
QM151 .F76 2001
612.7′4—dc21
                                    00-025178

Note to Parents and Teachers

The Human Body Systems series supports national science standards for units on understanding the basic functions of the human body. This book describes the muscular system and illustrates its purpose, parts, and functions. The photographs and diagrams support early readers in understanding the text. This book also introduces early readers to subject-specific vocabulary words, which are defined in the Words to Know section. Early readers may need assistance to read some words and to use the Table of Contents, Words to Know, Read More, Internet Sites, and Index/Word List sections of the book.

Table of Contents

The muscular system helps the body move. Different muscles move different parts of the body.

Most muscles work in pairs. One muscle contracts when the other muscle relaxes. This action causes a part of the body to move.

Legs have many pairs of large muscles. Leg muscles help people jump.

Small muscles in the hands work together. Hand muscles help people draw.

Small muscles in the face work together. Face muscles help people smile.

Some muscles work all the time. The heart is a muscle. It pumps blood through the body.

Sometimes many muscles in the body work together. People use many muscles when they swim.

Exercise keeps muscles healthy. Muscles grow stronger when they are used.

Words to Know

contract—to tighten; a muscle becomes shorter when it contracts; this causes part of the body to move.

exercise—activity that keeps people fit and healthy; exercise uses muscles and makes them stronger.

healthy—fit and well; healthy muscles are strong.

heart—a body part inside the chest; the heart pumps blood through the body; the heart is a muscle that works all the time.

muscle—a body part that produces movement

pump—to force a liquid or gas from one place to another

relax—to loosen; a muscle becomes longer when it relaxes.

Read More

Ballard, Carol. *How Do We Move?* How Your Body Works. Austin, Texas: Raintree Steck-Vaughn, 1998.

Llamas, Andreu. *Muscles and Bones.* The Human Body. Milwaukee: Gareth Stevens, 1998.

Simon, Seymour. *Muscles: Our Muscular System.* New York: Morrow Junior Books, 1998.

Internet Sites

The Bundles of Energy—The Muscular System
http://infozone.imcpl.org/kids_musc.htm

Your Gross and Cool Body—Muscular System
http://yucky.kids.discovery.com/noflash/body/pg00123.html

Your Multi-talented Muscles
http://kidshealth.org/kid/body/muscles_noSW.html

Index/Word List

arms, 11
back, 11
blood, 17
body, 5, 7, 17, 19
contracts, 7
exercise, 21
face, 15
hands, 13
healthy, 21
heart, 17

leg, 9
move, 5, 7
muscles, 5, 7, 9, 11, 13, 15, 17, 19, 21
muscular system, 5
pairs, 7, 9
part, 5, 7
people, 9, 11, 13, 15, 19
relaxes, 7

Word Count: 131
Early-Intervention Level: 16

Editorial Credits
Martha E. H. Rustad, editor; Kia Bielke, designer; Marilyn Moseley LaMantia, Graphicstock, illustrator; Katy Kudela, photo researcher

Photo Credits
David F. Clobes, cover, 20
Index Stock Imagery, 18
International Stock/Dusty Willison, 1
Marilyn Moseley LaMantia, 6, 10, 12, 16
Photo Network/Myrleen Ferguson Cate, 14
Pictor, 4; Jeffry W. Myers/Pictor, 8

The author thanks the children's section staff at the Allen County Public Library in Fort Wayne, Indiana, for research assistance. The author also thanks Linda Hathaway, CFCS, Health Educator, McMillen Center for Health Education, Fort Wayne, Indiana.